W9-CDO-206

A2.0.5

EXPLORING DINOSAURS

DIPLODOCUS

By Susan H. Gray

THE CHILD'S WORLD®
CHANHASSEN, MINNESOTA

The Child's World

Published in the United States of America by The Child's World®
PO Box 326, Chanhassen, MN 55317-0326
800-599-READ
www.childsworld.com

Photo Credits: American Museum of Natural History: 13, 15, 17, 24; Animals Animals/Earth Scenes/Scott W. Smith: 25; Corbis: 6, 12 (Darrell Gulin), 16 (George D. Lepp), 20 (Hulton-Deutsch Collection); Getty Images/Time Life Pictures: 8; Michael Skrepnick: 5, 10, 23; Mike Fredericks: 9, 11; Photo Researchers: 21 (Science Photo Library/Ludek Pesek), 27 (Joyce Photo); Todd Marshall: 26; Underwood & Underwood/Corbis: 18, 19.

*Content Adviser:
Peter Makovicky,
Ph.D., Curator,
Field Museum,
Chicago, Illinois*

The Child's World®: Mary Berendes, Publishing Director

Editorial Directions, Inc.: E. Russell Primm, Editorial Director; Ruth M. Martin, Line Editor; Katie Marsico, Assistant Editor; Matthew Messbarger, Editorial Assistant; Susan Hindman, Copy Editor; Susan Ashley, Proofreader; Tim Griffin, Indexer; Kerry Reid, Fact Checker; Cian Loughlin O'Day, Photo Researcher; Linda S. Koutris, Photo Selector

Original cover art by Todd Marshall

The Design Lab: Kathleen Petelinsek, Design and Art Direction; Kari Thornborough, Page Production

Library of Congress Cataloging-in-Publication Data
Gray, Susan Heinrichs.
  Diplodocus / by Susan H. Gray.
    p. cm. — (Exploring dinosaurs)
Includes index.
Contents: Just finishing dinner—What is a Diplodocus?—Who found the first Diplodocus?—Were there more than one?—What was life like for Diplodocus—When did Diplodocus live?
  ISBN 1-59296-186-X (lib. bdg. : alk. paper)
  1. Diplodocus—Juvenile literature. [1. Diplodocus. 2. Dinosaurs.] I. Title. II. Series.
QE862.S3G694 2004
567.913—dc22   2003018625

TABLE OF CONTENTS

JAN.   2007

CHAPTER ONE

JUST FINISHING DINNER

Diplodocus (dih-PLOD-uh-kuss) was having a great meal.

He stood at the edge of the forest with his long neck reaching deep into the shade. He turned his head to the right and tore a low branch from a tree. He worked it around in his mouth for a few seconds, then swallowed it whole.

Next, he swung his neck to the left. He bit down on a little bush, then jerked his head back. The bush ripped from the ground. *Diplodocus* downed it in one gulp.

Then he spied his favorite food—ferns—straight in front of him. *Diplodocus* took a step forward, then stopped cold. He couldn't move another inch. He was stuck. He turned his head to see what was wrong. Thirty feet (9 meters) behind his

Diplodocus was a dinosaur that really loved to eat. It had to eat a lot of food every single day to survive. It could swallow whole branches! Diplodocus *also swallowed stones called gastroliths that helped it grind down all that tough plant material.*

head, he could see his huge shoulders jammed tightly between

two trees.

Diplodocus heaved forward, straining to reach the ferns. The

trees creaked, but barely moved. He relaxed for a second, then

pushed forward again. One tree began to lean away just a little

bit. *Diplodocus* breathed heavily now and his huge heart pounded.

Ferns were a plentiful plant when Diplodocus *lived. A hungry* Diplodocus *could gulp down a lot of ferns—it had a large stomach to fill! Conifers (cone-bearing trees and shrubs) were probably its main snack.*

He strained forward a third time. The tree shook and fell over to the side. *Diplodocus* stumbled forward, ramming his face into the ferns. Soft, tender ferns—just what he wanted. *Diplodocus* quickly finished his meal, backed out of the forest, and looked for a place to catch a nap.

CHAPTER TWO

WHAT IS A DIPLODOCUS?

Diplodocus is a dinosaur that lived from about 150 million to 144 million years ago. Its name is taken from Greek words that mean "double beam." A beam is a strong structure that holds up something. For *Diplodocus,* the double beam refers to a series of bones that grew underneath its backbone and down through its tail. The bones helped support the tail muscles and protected the tail's blood vessels.

Diplodocus was an incredibly huge **reptile.** It was one of the largest land creatures to ever exist on Earth. From its snout to the tip of its tail, the typical adult *Diplodocus* was about 85 feet (26 m) long. Some even reached a length of

Diplodocus was incredibly long, with feet and legs similar to those of an elephant. This indicates that it was either a land or a swamp dweller.

100 feet (30 m). An animal that size would be about the same length as two trailer trucks parked end to end!

The giant dinosaur's neck and body made up about half of its length. Its long tail made up the other half. A single row of short spines ran down the dinosaur's back and tail.

Diplodocus had a little head for its size. The animal's activities and movements were controlled by a brain the size of an orange. A cluster of nerve cells at the base of its tail was a little bigger than its brain. Scientists once thought these nerve cells might be a second brain. Now they think they may have controlled the movements of the dinosaur's back legs and tail.

The reptile's nostrils were high up on its head. Its mouth had teeth only in the front. Shaped like big, blunt pencils, they

Though Diplodocus *was one of the longest dinosaurs, it had one of the smallest brains. It was among the least intelligent of all dinosaurs.*

were good for tearing plant material from trees or from the ground. The animal did not have back teeth for chewing and grinding food. It probably swallowed its food whole.

Because its nostrils were located high up on its head, scientists once thought that Diplodocus *lived on the bottom of lakes with only the top of its head above the water.*

Diplodocus's gigantic legs were like tree trunks. Its back legs were longer than its front legs, so the dinosaur's back sloped down from the hips to the shoulders. Each foot was broad and had five toes.

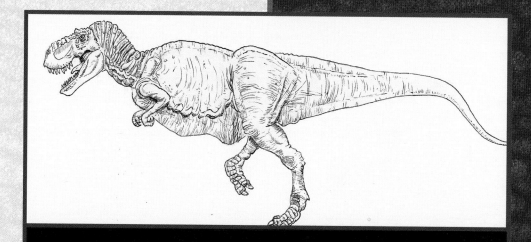

THE DINOSAUR WEIGHT PROBLEM

Scientists often tell us how much they believe a dinosaur weighed. They say, for example, that *Diplodocus* weighed between 10 and 15 tons. They say that *Tyranno-saurus rex* (tie-RAN-uh-SORE-uhss REX) weighed around 6 or 7 tons. They tell us that *Oviraptor* (OH-vih-RAP-tur) weighed about 55 to 75 pounds. But no one has ever weighed these dinosaurs. All we have are the dinosaurs' skeletons. So how does anyone know how much a dinosaur really weighed?

Scientists do several things to figure out a dino-saur's weight. First, they look at the animal's skele-ton. Suppose the skeleton shows that the dinosaur was wide, built low to the ground, and walked on all four feet. This was proba-bly the skeleton of a big, chunky, slow-moving dinosaur that had huge, strong legs. The dinosaur

might have been built somewhat like a rhinoceros of today.

Suppose another skeleton shows that the dinosaur had lightweight bones, a narrow skull, and moved around on two legs. This was probably the skeleton of a slender, quick, and agile dinosaur. It might have been built more like a modern ostrich.

Scientists often study modern animals and use this knowledge to understand dinosaurs. They might figure out what a rhinoceros or ostrich would weigh if it were the size of those dinosaurs. Then they can decide how that weight would compare to the weight of the actual dinosaur. As scientists learn more about each dinosaur, they can adjust its weight up or down. Of course, no one really knows exactly how much *Diplodocus* or any other dinosaur weighed. We can only make good guesses.

CHAPTER THREE

WHO FOUND THE FIRST DIPLODOCUS?

n 1877, Samuel Williston became the first person to discover *Diplodocus*. He worked with Othniel Charles Marsh, a famous paleontologist (PAY-lee-un-TAWL-uh-jist). Paleontologists are people who study plants and animals that lived

Samuel Williston was a paleontologist who specialized in reptiles that lived millions of years ago. He was also a dipterologist (DIP-ter-AWL-uh-jist) (someone who studies flies), medical doctor, author, and professor. He was Othniel Marsh's assistant at the Yale Peabody Museum from 1876 to 1890.

millions of years ago. They look for **fossils** of these **ancient**

living things.

In the late 1800s, dinosaurs were quite popular. Everyone

wanted to know about these mysterious creatures. Teams of paleon-

tologists went all over the western United States to hunt for dinosaur

bones. Every little discovery became big news. Dinosaurs were in all

of the newspapers.

Othniel Charles Marsh was one of the most famous dinosaur hunt-

ers of the time. He and his workers discovered dozens of new dino-

saurs. Their discovery of *Diplodocus* was especially spectacular. As the

longest dinosaur ever found, it captured everyone's attention. It even

caught the attention of Andrew Carnegie, one of the richest men in

the world. Carnegie sent some of his own workers to hunt for dinosaur

fossils. In 1899 and 1900, they discovered even more *Diplodocus* bones.

Since that time, a few more *Diplodocus* discoveries have been made. You might think that many skeletons of the huge dinosaur have been found. But this is not the case. Altogether, paleontologists have found only a few skeletons, a few skulls, and some backbones.

Othniel Marsh was an American paleontologist from Yale University who named around 500 new species of fossil animals. These fossils were discovered by Marsh and his fossil hunters on their many expeditions. Marsh named the dinosaur suborder of Sauropoda, of which Diplodocus *was a member.*

Still, this is enough to teach us a lot about this ancient giant.

MORE THAN ONE?

Like most dinosaurs, there were several different kinds of *Diplodocus*. Each kind has its own name. Scientists usually give animals two special names. The first is called the genus (JEE-nuss) name. The second is called the species (SPEE-seez) name. These two names tell us something about the animal.

Animals with the same genus name are very much alike. But there are still some differences. For example, house cats and mountain lions have the same genus name. They are both catlike animals, and are

Mountain lions have many names besides their special scientific ones. People also call them cougars, pumas, and panthers.

enough alike to share the genus name *Felis.* But they are also different enough to have different species names. The house cat is named *Felis catus,* and the mountain lion is *Felis concolor.*

It is the same way with dinosaurs. *Diplodocus* is the genus name for the dinosaurs that were "double-beamed." But there were different kinds of double-beamed dinosaurs.

The very first *Diplodocus* ever found is now called *Diplodocus longus* (LONG-guss), meaning "long double-beam." Years later, *Diplodocus carnegii* (kar-NEG-ee-eye) was

Walter Granger was one of the world's most famous paleontologists. He traveled all over the world collecting fossils. It was in Wyoming that he found a huge bed of dinosaur remains, including those of Diplodocus.

Dr. Barnum Brown discovered these Diplodocus longus *in the early 1930's on a dig in Howe Quarry, Wyoming. Brown was most famous for his discovery of the* Tyrannosaurus rex *in 1902.*

found. This was a double-beamed dinosaur named after Andrew Carnegie, the man who hired the team that discovered it. Its bones were a little different from the bones of *Diplodocus longus.*

A few years later, *Diplodocus hayi* (HAY-eye) was found. Its bones were also unique. It was named after the scientist Oliver Hay. All of these dinosaurs were alike enough to share the name *Diplodocus.* But their bones showed that they were not exactly alike. They were just different enough to receive different names.

DIPPY SEES THE WORLD

One morning in 1898, Andrew Carnegie opened his newspaper and could not believe what he read. The headline screamed, "Most Colossal Animal Ever on Earth Just Found Out West!" Someone in Wyoming had discovered part of a gigantic dinosaur. Carnegie knew he had to have one for his museum.

He sent men out to search the area. Weeks, then months passed. Finally, on July 4, 1899, they discovered the bones of a *Diplodocus*. More discoveries followed, and the men sent crate after crate of bones back to the museum. As museum workers pieced the skeleton together, they saw *Diplodocus* stretch to more than 80 feet (24 m) in length.

The King of England soon heard about the giant

creature and wanted one
for his country. So Carnegie's workers made a cast,
or copy, of every bone,
brought them to London,
and put them together.
When the dinosaur was
shown to the public,
everyone went wild.
They nicknamed it Dippy
and came from miles
around to see it. Dippy
was so popular that
someone even wrote
a song about it!

The dinosaur's fame
spread all over the world.
Soon, the leaders of Ger-
many, France, Italy, Spain,
Russia, and Argentina
wanted their own Dippy.
Carnegie's workers kept
making copies until everyone was satisfied.

Thousands of people
came to see the skeletons.
In France, the crowds
shouted, "Vive le Dippy!"
which meant, "Long live
Dippy!" when they saw
the dinosaur. Other coun-
tries printed up post-
cards of the creature.
It had been 150 million
years since the dinosaur
roamed the land that
became Wyoming. Now
Dippy was traveling
the world.

CHAPTER FIVE

WHAT WAS LIFE LIKE FOR
DIPLODOCUS?

What would a typical day be like for an animal that was as big as two trailer trucks? Most of it would be spent eating. This is probably just what *Diplodocus* did.

Scientists agree that *Diplodocus* was a plant eater, or herbivore (UR-buh-vore). But they do not agree on just how the reptile got its food. Did it reach up to eat from tall trees? Did it rear up on its hind

The Jurassic period is named for the Jura Mountains that lie between France and Switzerland. Rocks from the Jurassic period were first discovered and studied here.

legs and lean back on its tail? Did it stand in one place, swinging its head around to eat everything on the ground? Did it stand on dry ground while its head reached for food in swampy areas?

The dinosaur may have done all of these things. But some ways of eating might have been more difficult than others. For one thing, lifting its head up high could have caused problems. If *Diplodocus* stretched its neck to eat from the treetops, its head might have been as high as 30 feet (9 m) above the ground. The dinosaur's heart would have had to pump very hard to move blood all that way up to the brain. Scientists aren't sure *Diplodocus*'s heart was strong enough to do that. So perhaps the dinosaur just ate plants that were low to the ground.

At times, *Diplodocus* probably became a meal for some other dinosaur. The fierce *Allosaurus* (AL-oh-SORE-uhss) lived at the

Because Diplodocus *was so large, it might have been able to fight off its enemies, such as the* Allosaurus *pictured here. However, some scientists think* Allosuarus *may have hunted in packs, in which case they could have easily ambushed an unsuspecting* Diplodocus.

same time and place as *Diplodocus.* Its muscular jaws and sharp

teeth could inflict **mortal** wounds on the big plant eater. However,

Diplodocus had a long, whiplike tail. It was powerful, flexible, and

could knock an attacker senseless. Plus, one good stomp from

Diplodocus's foot could end the life of any **predator.** *Diplodocus*

might have looked like an easy target, but it wasn't helpless!

CHAPTER SIX

WHEN DID
DIPLODOCUS LIVE?

Diplodocus lived during a time span called the Jurassic

(jer-RASS-ik) period. This was a stretch of time from

about 208 million to 144 million years ago. During this period,

Earth was warmer than it is today. In fact, the North and South

Poles were not even covered with ice as they are now. Temperatures

at the poles were cool, but not freezing cold.

*A mass extinction happened at the end of the Triassic period, which
gave way to an abundance of dinosaurs during the Jurassic period.*

Ginkgoes are a type of tree that originated in eastern China. They are usually grown as ornaments or for shade. They are known not just for their fan-shaped leaves, but also for their smelly yellow seed coatings.

Many places on Earth were warm and damp. In western North America, where *Diplodocus* lived, plants were plentiful. Sticklike plants called horsetails grew in marshy areas. Ginkgo trees waved their fanlike leaves in the breezes. The stiff leaves of cycads (SY-kadz) rattled each time the wind blew. Soft mosses carpeted the ground, and ferns were everywhere.

This was a time when dinosaurs ruled the Earth. All over the world, giant plant-eaters and fierce meat-eaters roamed. Flying reptiles swooped overhead. Water-loving reptiles swam the rivers and oceans.

Yikes! The Jurassic seas were full of huge sea predators, such as marine crocodiles, dolphinlike ichthyosaurs (IK-thee-oh-sawrz), and long-necked plesiosaurs (PLEE-zee-oh-sawrz). Plesiosaurs had barrel-shaped bodies and diamond-shaped flippers.

This is a picture of the tail vertebrae of a Diplodocus. *Besides its long neck, the* Diplodocus *had an extremely long tail. The tail had 80 or more vertebrae, including 19 hollow vertebrae that were close to the hips.*

Diplodocus died out just as the Jurassic period was ending. Eighty million years later, all of the dinosaurs were gone. And 65 million years after that, the first *Diplodocus* bones were discovered in Wyoming. It's too bad those bones cannot talk. They could tell us everything about *Diplodocus*—how it lived, and why it died.

Glossary

agile (AJ-ill) Something that is agile can move easily. *Dilpodocus* was probably not very agile.

ancient (AYN-shunt) Something that is ancient is very old; from millions of years ago. Fossils give us clues about ancient creatures, such as dinosaurs.

fossils (FOSS-uhlz) Fossils are the remains of ancient plants and animals. Scientists study fossils to learn about life on Earth millions of years ago.

mortal (MOR-tuhl) A mortal wound is a wound that causes death. *Diplodocus* could give another dinosaur a mortal injury using only its foot.

predator (PRED-uh-tor) A predator is an animal that hunts and eats other animals. *Diplodocus* had to be careful of predators that would try to kill it.

reptile (REP-tile) A reptile is an air-breathing animal with a backbone and is usually covered with scales or plates. *Diplodocus* was a reptile.

Did You Know?

▸ *Diplodocus* is no longer known as the longest dinosaur. Other dinosaurs, such as *Seismosaurus* (SIZE-moh-SORE-uhss), were much longer.

▸ When newspapers printed that the "most colossal animal" had been found, they were cheating a little. At the time, someone had found only part of the dinosaur's leg bone.

▸ Paleontologists working for Andrew Carnegie found a *Diplodocus* in Wyoming on July 4, 1899. Some of them called it the star-spangled dinosaur.

The Geologic Time Scale

TRIASSIC PERIOD

Date: 248 million to 208 million years ago

Fossils: *Coelophysis, Cynodont, Desmatosuchus, Eoraptor, Gerrothorax, Peteinosaurus, Placerias, Plateosaurus, Postosuchus, Procompsognathus, Riojasaurus, Saltopus, Teratosaurus, Thecodontosaurus*

Distinguishing Features: For the most part, the climate in the Triassic period was hot and dry. The first true mammals appeared during this period, as well as turtles, frogs, salamanders, and lizards. Corals could also be found in oceans at this time, although large reefs such as the ones we have today did not yet exist. Evergreen trees made up much of the plant life. At the end of the Triassic period, there was a mass extinction. 35% of animal families died out.

JURASSIC PERIOD

Date: 208 million to 144 million years ago

Fossils: *Allosaurus, Anchisaurus, Apatosaurus, Barosaurus, Brachiosaurus, Ceratosaurus, Compsognathus, Cryptoclidus, Dilophosaurus, Diplodocus, Eustreptospondylus, Hybodus, Janenschia, Kentrosaurus, Liopleurodon, Megalosaurus, Opthalmosaurus, Rhamphorhynchus, Saurolophus, Segisaurus, Seismosaurus, Stegosaurus, Supersaurus, Syntarsus, Ultrasaurus, Vulcanodon, Xiaosaurus*

Distinguishing Features: The climate of the Jurassic period was warm and moist. The first birds appeared during this period. Plant life was also greener and more widespread. Sharks began swimming in Earth's oceans. Although dinosaurs didn't even exist at the beginning of the Triassic period, they ruled Earth by Jurassic times. There was a minor mass extinction toward the end of the Jurassic period.

CRETACEOUS PERIOD

Date: 144 million to 65 million years ago

Fossils: *Acrocanthosaurus, Alamosaurus, Albertosaurus, Anatotitan, Ankylosaurus, Argentinosaurus, Bagaceratops, Baryonyx, Carcharodontosaurus, Carnotaurus, Centrosaurus, Chasmosaurus, Corythosaurus, Didelphodon, Edmontonia, Edmontosaurus, Gallimimus, Gigantosaurus, Hadrosaurus, Hypsilophodon, Iguanodon, Kronosaurus, Lambeosaurus, Leaellynasaura, Maiasaura, Megaraptor, Muttaburrasaurus, Nodosaurus, Ornithocheirus, Oviraptor, Pachycephalosaurus, Panoplosaurus, Parasaurolophus, Pentaceratops, Polacanthus, Protoceratops, Psittacosaurus, Quaesitosaurus, Saltasaurus, Sarcosuchus, Saurolophus, Sauropelta, Saurornithoides, Segnosaurus, Spinosaurus, Stegoceras, Stygimoloch, Styracosaurus, Tapejara, Tarbosaurus, Therizinosaurus, Thescelosaurus, Torosaurus, Trachodon, Triceratops, Troodon, Tyrannosaurus rex, Utahraptor, Velociraptor*

Distinguishing Features: The climate of the Cretaceous period was fairly mild. Flowering plants first appeared in this period, and many modern plants developed. With flowering plants came a greater diversity of insect life. Birds further developed into two types: flying and flightless. A wider variety of mammals also existed. At the end of this period came a great mass extinction that wiped out the dinosaurs, along with several other groups of animals.

How to Learn More

At the Library

Holtz, Thomas R., Jr., Michael Brett-Surman, and Robert Walters (illustrator). *Dinosaur Field Guide: Jurassic Park Institute.* New York: Random House, 2001.

Lambert, David, Darren Naish, and Liz Wyse. *Dinosaur Encyclopedia.* New York: DK Publishing, 2001.

On the Web

Visit our home page for lots of links about *Diplodocus:*
http://www.childsworld.com/links.html
Note to Parents, Teachers, and Librarians: We routinely verify our
Web links to make sure they're safe, active sites—so encourage
your readers to check them out!

Places to Visit or Contact

AMERICAN MUSEUM OF NATURAL HISTORY
To view numerous dinosaur fossils, as well
as the fossils of several ancient mammals
Central Park West at 79th Street
New York, NY 10024-5192
212/769-5100

CARNEGIE MUSEUM OF NATURAL HISTORY
To see Dippy, a Diplodocus *skeleton*
4400 Forbes Avenue
Pittsburgh, PA 15213
412/622-3131

DINOSAUR NATIONAL MONUMENT
To view a huge deposit of dinosaur bones in a natural setting
Dinosaur, CO 81610-9724
or
Dinosaur National Monument (Quarry)
11625 East 1500 South
Jensen, UT 84035
435/781-7700

MUSEUM OF THE ROCKIES
To see real dinosaur fossils, as well as robotic replicas
Montana State University
600 West Kagy Boulevard
Bozeman, MT 59717-2730
406/994-2251 or 406/994-DINO (3466)

NATIONAL MUSEUM OF NATURAL HISTORY
(SMITHSONIAN INSTITUTION)
To see several dinosaur exhibits and special behind-the-scenes tours
10th Street and Constitution Avenue, N.W.
Washington, D.C. 20560-0166
202/357-2700

Index

About the Author

Susan H. Gray has bachelor's and master's degrees in zoology, and has taught college-level courses in biology. She first fell in love with fossil hunting while studying paleontology in college. In her 25 years as an author, she has written many articles for scientists and researchers, and many science books for children. Susan enjoys gardening, traveling, and playing the piano. She and her husband, Michael, live in Cabot, Arkansas.